Dr Catherine Stodda

CRISIS STEWARDSHIP

What do leaders need to take action in a crisis?

Publisher's Note

Every possible effort has been made to ensure that the information contained in this book is accurate at the time of going to press, and the publishers and authors cannot accept responsibility for any errors or omissions, however caused.

No responsibility for loss or damage occasioned to any person acting, or refraining from action, as a result of the material in this publication can be accepted by the editor, the publisher, or the author.

First edition published in the United Kingdom in 2024 by Ideas for Leaders Publishing, a business of IEDP Ideas for Leaders Ltd.

Apart from any fair dealing for the purposes of research or private study, or criticism or review, as permitted under the Copyright, Design and Patents Act 1988, this publication may only be reproduced, stored or transmitted, in any form or by any means, with the prior permission in writing of the publishers. Enquiries concerning reproduction should be sent to the publishers at the following address:

Ideas for Leaders Publishing
42 Moray Place
Edinburgh
EH3 6BT
www.ideasforleaders.com
info@ideasforleaders.com

ISBN
978-1-915529-32-9 – Paperback

978-1-915529-33-6 – E-book

*To Blake, Brodie, Fran and Mum
who have always cheered me on
from the sides, and Dr Helen Scott for her
patience and guidance.*

Thankyou

This book is based on the research from the author's doctoral thesis, submitted to Business Science Institute in 2023 as part of the requirements for the degree of Doctorate in Business Administration. The thesis was entitled, Crisis Stewards: Taking Action in Crisis - A Grounded Theory Study of Australian Public Sector Executives.

CONTENTS

Chapter 1

INTRODUCTION AND CONTEXT

The COVID-19 virus caused by SARS-CoV-2 spread across the globe like a wave, emerging from Wuhan, sweeping west across China, Russia and Europe to North and South America, and west through Asia, southeast Asia to Australia and New Zealand. In March 2020, the World Health Organization (WHO) declared that the virus had reached pandemic proportions. Global anxiety about the impact of the disease continued to rise as more and more people began to die. Nations around the world hurried to make significant changes to stop the further spread of the disease.

But it seemed the disease could not be stopped. It spread to nearly every country in the world. Within a year, according to WHO, more than 669 million confirmed cases had been reported worldwide, leading to more than 6.76 million deaths.

National leaders and decision makers had to take action, but what action to take with a new threat even the experts in infectious disease were struggling to understand? Working with public health officials and drawing on any other public sector and private sector insight and experience – for the impact was a public health issue, significantly disrupting the global economy and daily life – public sector leaders tried to act in the best interests of their citizens as they tried to slow the spread of the virus.

Some of these measures taken by governments around the world to reduce the economic and health impact of COVID-19 included:

- Implementing lockdowns and other restrictions on movement and crowd gatherings – impacting the workplace as employees in many sectors could not report to work, and the education sector, as students could not attend school.
- Providing financial support through direct payments, loans and grants to individuals and businesses affected by the pandemic.
- Increasing healthcare spending and resources to help hospitals and healthcare workers overwhelmed by the influx of patients – many of them resistant to the idea of the virus.
- Working with pharmaceutical companies to fast-track the development and distribution of vaccines to help curb the spread of the virus.

The societal impact was so deep and profound that even these measures were not enough. Governments needed to take steps to stabilise financial markets and prevent widespread economic collapse; they did so by providing financial support to large multi-nationals and implementing interest rate reductions.

Countries are different, and any measures taken had to be tailored to the specific circumstances of each country. In addition, the responses had to be adjusted as new information and new iterations of the virus emerged. Yet, there was at the same time recurring themes and approaches in the response by the public sectors and administrations in the many different countries. The streets and sports stadiums in cities and towns across the globe were emptied as governments introduced lockdowns and social distancing measures to prevent the spread of COVID-19.

What I've just described is the context of the years 2020 and 2021, which is when the research at the heart of this book was conducted. For it is in these two years that public sector leaders faced the most intense pressure to manage the response and expectations of the citizens of their nations. Although outbreaks continue to occur across the world, on May 5, 2023 WHO declared that COVID -19 no longer constituted a public health emergency of international concern (PHEIC), (WHO 2023). As I write this in 2024, the management of COVID-19 has become somewhat normalized, though governments and public sector leaders around the world continue to make decisions and shape strategies to reduce the impact of COVID-19 and its effect on citizens.

The Australian Experience

In Australia, COVID-19 did not wreak the kind of havoc seen in many of the other Organisation for Economic Cooperation and Development (OECD) countries. There were significantly lower numbers of cases and deaths per capita. In January 2020, 243 Australian citizens returned from Wuhan and were sent to an Australian quarantine facility on Christmas Island just off the coast of Western Australia. As of January 2023, Australia, a nation of approximately 25 million people, had seen a total of 11.3 million cases of COVID-19, and 18,000 COVID-19-related deaths. As with many other countries, Australia prepared for the arrival of the disease, and when the outbreak manifested itself, responded with a number of steps and directives, notably by encouraging the wearing of masks, closing schools, restricting gatherings, and adjusting domestic and internal travel. While these steps may sound familiar, the application of these measures were severe and extensive – with the domestic and international travel restrictions among the most severe in the world, according to WHO. (Australia also provided financial support for unemployed people and small businesses to limit or at least reduce the impact on individuals and the economy.) Australia's unequivocal response to the pandemic had its rewards. Australia was one of the few countries in 2020 that was able to bring new cases of COVID-19 down to zero. Compared to many other countries, Australia has also been less impacted by subsequent waves of COVID-19.

Although the ultimate impact of COVID-19 was less intense than for other countries, no public leader at any level of the nation was spared from dealing with the pandemic. Responding to the crisis required, at the national level, leaders to make difficult and often politically controversial decisions, such as implementing lockdowns, managing the distribution of vaccines and other measures to slow the spread of the virus. These decisions were often met with criticism levelled at some leaders by the public. At the state and local levels, public leaders managed the response to the pandemic in their state or communities – a response that included communicating information to the public and working with other organizations and agencies. One important partner for public sector leaders was the media. which played an important role in shaping the public information emanating from these leaders in Australia. Despite the quick turnover of the decisions and the inconsistent information about the disease that changed over time as more information became available, the press helped the general public have confidence in the decisions being taken by the local and state political leaders (Nolan et al. 2021). Local and state public leaders also had to balance their response to ensure reducing the long-term economic impacts of the pandemic while still keeping enough resources required to address the more urgent needs, such as the distribution of personal protective equipment (PPE) and vaccines.

The Challenge for Public Sector Leaders

I am a registered nurse and at the time of the COVID-19 pandemic, I was a senior leader of an Australian government health agency with responsibility for overseeing the health response within a jurisdiction. The combination of my background in healthcare and my responsibilities as a public sector leader influenced my research interest in this area. I had experience managing crisis such as cyclones, power failures, and financial crises, but managing the COVID-19 response felt different. The community and the government expected the public sector to take a leadership role in responding to the pandemic, and held the public sector accountable for the results. As the crisis progressed, my efforts in responding to the crisis affected me personally but also professionally as a leader. I found that I had to rethink my leadership style as the urgent need to protect the community challenged my comfort with decision making and taking action. I wondered whether other public sector leaders had had a similar experience, and if this experience had influenced the way they responded to developments over the course of the pandemic.

I thus began to research the role of leaders in the public sector in the face of a sustained crisis. As defined by the Australian Public Sector Commission, public sector leaders are senior executives who 'are expected to lead by motivating and organizing people to produce outcomes that make a difference to the nation'. Since COVID-19 had required me, as a public servant, to modify and change my leadership style, I decided to investigate whether responding to the pandemic had the same effect on other public sector leaders in terms of their leadership roles and styles.

This book will describe the attributes and capabilities of public sector leaders (Schmidt et al., 2017; Schmidt et al 2021; Van Wart 2003) and how such attributes and capabilities – as well as other influences – influenced their response to the crisis of COVID-19.

To better understand the role of public sector leaders in Australia, it helps to know something about how the public sector in our country operates. There are three levels of government – federal, state (or territory), and local – that comprise the public sector in Australia. At all three of these levels, departments covering a range of functions, including health, police and community services, played an important role in responding to the COVID-19 pandemic, specifically in coordinating the emergency response in each state and territory through public health and emergency declarations. Importantly, the time frame in which these public sector agencies operated changed dramatically. Instead of focusing on strategic policy implementation and bureaucratic administration, they were suddenly required to implement an emergency response (Van Wart & Kapucu, 2011). Public sector leaders in the various departments stepped up to the task, providing leadership responses on behalf of the Australian Commonwealth Government and each of the state and territory governments across Australia. Among their responses: establishing quarantine and border controls; providing support for vulnerable groups, including businesses; putting in place required public health measures; and acquiring and distributing health resources and protective equipment, such as masks.

The condensed time frame in which public sector leaders needed to accept and fulfill their responsibilities cannot be overstated. In the face of continuous and rapidly changing circumstances, and the urgency of a response on which lives depended, these public sector leaders had to both provide expert advice to the government and then rapidly implement government policies or emergency decisions (Department of Health, 2021). The expert advice was based on epidemiological information and an assessment of emerging risks and led to decisions on social distancing as well as border restrictions and quarantine measures for incoming international travellers. As a leader in the public sector, I had to continuously monitor and review the changing situation, responding to each stage of the pandemic and striving to learn from my experience. This led me to research how other public sector leaders were impacted by this experience.

Impact of the Crisis on Public Sector Leaders

A crisis of the significance of the COVID-19 pandemic is, one might say thankfully, rare. The last time a health care crisis of this magnitude hit the globe was the Spanish flu of 1917. Thus, in terms of crisis leadership, COVID-19 offered a unique opportunity to explore the intersection of crisis leadership and public sector leadership, highlighting the importance of effective public leadership in responding to crises, managing risks, and ensuring the well-being of citizens (Boin et. al. 2005). The effectiveness of crisis leadership in this case rested in four areas:

- *Crisis management*: The public sector was the key player in managing the crisis caused by COVID-19. Its responsibilities included coordinating responses at local, state, and national levels, and working with the healthcare-related sectors to provide medical care and support to those affected by COVID-19.
- *Risk management*: Perhaps the greatest challenge of responding to the crisis, and one that fell squarely on the shoulders of public sector leaders, was managing the risk to citizens that the pandemic represented. In the case of weather-related crises, for example, one deals with managing the aftermath and with implementing preventive measures to mitigate the damage of similar future crises. The pandemic, however, was a moving target in which the breadth of the risk and the most appropriate response only became fully understood over time. The two pillars

of risk management were implementing measures, such as lockdowns and travel bans, to prevent the spread of the virus, and ensuring that citizens had access to the latest, most accurate information about the virus.

- *Citizens' welfare*: Ensuring the welfare of citizens is a core responsibility for public sector leaders. The pandemic created never-before-seen complications that leaders needed to overcome. For example, the level of financial support needed to support individuals and businesses affected by the crisis was unprecedented. Public sector leaders also found themselves working with organizations to ensure that even the most basic of needs, such as food and housing, were met.

- *Innovation in remote and new ways of working and service*: There is one area in which the challenge presented to the public sector by the pandemic transcended the sector. The private sector found itself with the challenge of continuing to run their businesses while unable to bring employees into the workplace. The public sector found itself with the same challenge, which led to public organizations adapting to new ways of working, based on remote work and online services. Only through these new ways of working could public organizations continue to fulfill their core functions of providing essential services to citizens while avoiding exacerbating the risk of the spread of the virus.

Overall, the COVID-19 pandemic tested the nature of the public leaders' role, their accountability and their leadership skills. Never in their experience had public leaders been forced to make such impactful decisions so quickly and under greater scrutiny before. Never before had the decisions of these leaders been so closely monitored by the media and the general public. Never had the evaluation of their actions and decisions ranged so widely from highly critical to highly supportive. The response to these decisions and actions, on the part of the media especially, varied depending on the area being addressed, such as weather, healthcare, the police service or a core agency such as finance and infrastructure. I was interested in exploring how the crisis affected leadership style to manage this multitude of challenges.

What is the Public Sector in Australia?

Public sector leaders are the leaders and managers of the public servants who provide policy, services, regulations or standards. The organizations and agencies of Australia's public sector, which as noted earlier are present at federal, state or territory, and local level, are led by the hierarchy of the government, from the national leader, the heads of the state governments and the leaders of the governing political parties, and the heads of various departments and agencies, such as the Department of Health, the Department of Education and the Department of Treasury. The management and performance of the public sector is monitored by the Public Sector Commission. Public sector leaders can be appointed by the government in power at the time, or through a merit-based selection process (Australian Public Sector Commission, 2021).

During the pandemic, the responsibilities of public sector agencies was two-fold. First, they were charged with providing expert advice to the government based on acquired or emerging information as well as the expert advice from those with technical expertise and experience in such areas as public health or border control. Their second task was to implement as quickly as possible government policies or urgent emergency decisions (Department of Health, 2021). For example, public sector leaders in the agencies provided advice to government on issues that could range from something as specific as the suggested distance for people to maintain between each other in public to broader issues, such as how to manage environmental health issues or the impact of the pandemic on homeless individuals. All of these decisions could not have been more impactful since they affected jobs, tourism, industry businesses, and the broader community.

Public Sector Leadership Response to Crisis

Because the pandemic was characterized by both continuously changing circumstances and the intensely urgent need for action, public sector leaders had to change their focus if they were to successfully reduce the impact of the crisis. The once strategy-heavy focus of public leadership transformed into a more complex focus on both strategic and tactical considerations simultaneously. They needed to continue providing and implementing strategic policy advice, with bureaucratic oversight that was perhaps stronger than usual; at the same time, they now had a tactical role in implementing and delivering an emergency response (Van Wart & Kapucu, 2011).

Public sector leaders were thus required to continuously review the changing situation, responding to each stage of the pandemic without fail; this bias for action, however, needed to be accompanied by learning from each experience. Public leaders also needed to balance the need for an immediate response with consideration of the long-term impact of their actions on the crisis. In addition, the wheels of the government needed to keep turning for life had not come to a standstill. In other words, public leaders needed to respond to an unprecedented (in their lives) crisis while continuing as much as possible, business as usual (BAU). One can imagine the difficulty of achieving this balance between the urgent requirement to manage the immediate, day-to-day response to the pandemic while also managing its outcomes (whether health or economic), the longer-term implications for public policy, and the long-term effects on the lives of people. I found reaching this balance particularly challenging, with my day-to-day strategic work pushed aside by the urgent gravity of the pandemic's impact. This experience led me to explore whether other public sector leaders had had a similar experience.

These challenging and unique characteristics

of the pandemic that I just described – notably the changing environment and the urgency involved – required all leaders, including the heads of agencies such as those in health (Boin & Lodge, 2021) to change their leadership style. Successful leadership in this context required situational leadership – a rapid and agile leadership style that enabled public sector leaders to move between different contexts and senses of urgency. I was thus inspired to investigate how other public sector leaders might have changed their leadership roles and style in response to the pandemic. It should be noted that although this book focuses on the public sector, the lessons it contains applies to the not-for-profit and private sectors, since such crises as the COVID-19 pandemic impacts all sectors.

In this book, I describe the experiences of public sector leaders responding to the pandemic. From these experiences, I have developed some key strategies not only for public sector leaders but organizations in other sectors too, for future crises.

Responding as a Steward

Stewardship represents a commitment to the success of an organization or of society in general and specifically a commitment to the welfare and success of the people within it. Society, a broad term, can refer in this general definition of stewardship to any slice of society – for example, a geographic slice such as a state or nation or a demographic slice such as children, the elderly, or any other demographic tranche. Stewardship is at the heart of a public sector leader's function since they are responsible for the welfare and success of the people affected by the agency or governmental organization for which they work This book aims to describe the factors that can affect public sector leaders in providing a stewardship response to crises such as COVID-19. The initial stewardship function of these leaders is to protect society, but the COVID-19 pandemic required them to change their approach to protection from one of preventive strategies to tactical, emergency responses. This book reveals how and why different public sector leaders respond differently in crisis situations. Specifically, I explore the factors that impact a public sector leader's response, notably the power or authority of that leader to act, the capability of that leader to act (which depends on personal and leadership characteristics and styles) and the nature of the crisis itself. Ultimately, this book creates a framework that describes which public sector leaders will be more effective in meeting the needs of their communities in crisis situations and why.

Taking Action Successfully

The role of public sector leaders is to administer government policy and services, providing stewardship for citizens in the strategic development and implementation of policy (Public Sector Commission, 2020). This core stewardship role continues during a crisis but is more focused on resolving an imminent threat rather than anticipating a future one.

In this book I seek to explain how public sector leaders are able to take action in crisis to fulfil their role as stewards. I also dive into the factors that influence how much of an effective impact they are able to have on the outcome of the crisis. One factor is the authority given by the government to take action in the face of the threat. What I call *the power to act* is not solely dependent on government authors. As I will show the public discourse supporting action can also impact a leader's power to act. For example, public support for a robust response enabled public sector leaders to take stronger action; in contrast, public resistance to governmental response to the crisis – such as the anti-mask movement during the COVID-19 crisis – undermined the public sector leaders' power to act.

I will also explore the factors that influence a leader's *capacity to act*, which depends greatly on an individual's preferred leadership style and their personal experience with a crisis. Finally, organizational factors, such as the culture of the organization and the teams within that organization, can greatly impact an individual's ability to take action.

This book addresses these issues in the context of an unpredictable and persistent crisis that creates the need for action. The framework presented in the book will show how these factors will determine whether a public sector leader's actions can have a broad, societal impact, a more restrained sector-wide impact, or, in the case of less effective leaders, an impact limited to the local level. This book shows that the capability of public sector leaders to achieve the level of impact required in a large-scale crisis is influenced by individual, organizational, and system-level aspects. (Bentzen, 2021; Lui et al., 2022).

The ultimate framework that emerged from my study, called *Crisis Stewards – Taking Action in Crisis* brings together the characteristics of the crisis itself combined with the range of influencing factors that together create the *combined force* to take action. The typology of stewards described in Chapter Four reflects the combination of each of these elements. Since these influencers are linked to scope – that is, their effectiveness at the local, sector, or societal level – future leaders in the public sector will have some guidelines to consider the type of Crisis Stewardship needed to achieve the actions and impact required depending on the characteristics of the crisis.

Research During the Pandemic

This book has its roots in my experience of the COVID-19 crisis, an experience that created a professional concern related to my role as a leader in the public sector healthcare field. Specifically, I struggled with how to guarantee the health protection of the community and staff in a crisis that created an imminent threat and constant uncertainty. I wanted to understand how I could resolve or reduce the deep concern and anxiety that I was feeling in the crisis, which led me to wonder about the experiences and perspectives of other public sector leaders. How had they coped with the crisis? How much were they able to make the right decisions during COVID-19?

I first began to think about these questions during the early stages of the pandemic. Even in these early stages, it was becoming increasingly clear that this would be an ongoing crisis, and that decisions would have to be made rapidly in an environment of high complexity, uncertainty, and ambiguity.

As the crisis progressed, I observed public sector leaders working to make sense of the crisis and manage the risk on behalf of citizens – but the increasing anxiety of these leaders was evident across all levels of the system. For many leaders, this was not the first crisis with potential risks to citizens that they had managed. Other significant crises, related to cyber-security or natural disasters, for example, had already crossed their desks. But COVID-19 was different in terms of the political and public discourse. There was no single and obvious response, as in dealing with the aftermath of a natural disaster, for example. There was no easy consensus on what action needed to be taken. In meetings and discussions with colleagues, I heard their concern over their leadership role in the crisis. I quickly realized it was important to explore how public sector leaders were managing in the crisis and what we could learn from their experiences. COVID-19 was a major crisis with tragic consequences. But I knew it was important to use the COVID-19 pandemic to learn how best public sector leaders could respond in the future to such impactful crises and fulfill their roles as stewards.

And so I began my research.

Chapter 2

THE METHODOLOGY

In this chapter, I describe the methodology I used to identify or develop the ideas and concepts that eventually led to the *Crisis Stewards – Taking Action in Crisis* framework. The goal of my research was to uncover, firstly, the *main concern of public sector leaders when managing crises such as COVID-19,* and second, *how they seek to address these concerns.*

This 'research question' emanated from my concern about how the COVID-19 pandemic affected leader behaviours and experiences, both at a professional and a personal level. This question emerged during the early stages of the pandemic, when it was still an early threat but had the potential to be ongoing. Through my own experience I knew that decisions were being made rapidly in the context of high levels of complexity, uncertainty, and ambiguity.

As the crisis progressed, I observed public sector leaders seeking to make sense of the crisis and manage the risk on behalf of citizens. While many leaders had previously managed other potential risks to citizens, such as cyber security and natural disasters, this crisis would be vastly different, notably in terms of the political and public discourse.

To answer these questions, I carefully considered what would be the most suitable methodology for a full research study. I deemed what academics call the "Classic Grounded Theory" (CGT) methodology to be the most appropriate research method for this study. Grounded Theory is structured and pragmatic: its purpose is to offer 'an inductive methodology with a distinctly practical purpose: to provide a theory that has the potential to explain, interpret and guide practice.' (Breckenridge & Jones, 2009 p 123).

As I briefly describe in this chapter, CGT helps researchers – through systematic rounds of coding (analyzing and categorizing individual data items) – to move from data to early concepts to more higher-level concepts and theories, and ultimately, to the final theory or framework that provides the answers they are seeking. Grounded theory guided me to become more conceptual and theoretical in my analyses and research findings by helping to make sense of the intricate interplay of the issues that rose to the surface through my research.

Through CGT, I was able to understand patterns of behaviour that are not easy to observe, including my own (an autoethnography approach to better understand my own main concern and personal experiences was part of the CGT process). One of the principles of CGT is to set aside any preconceptions. Concepts and theories should be allowed to emerge from the data and the subsequent analyses as captured in memos.

In addition to the interviews, the data for this thesis also included newsletters, policies, and documents as they emerged from a variety of sources during the crisis. The flexibility of CGT was important given the changing dynamic of COVID-19: researchers are encouraged to consider any data that adds to the research as it emerges. As Glaser (1998) put it, 'The briefest of comments to the lengthiest interview, written words in magazines, books and newspapers, documents, observations, biases of self and other, spurious variables or whatever else may come the researcher's way in substantive areas is [all] data for grounded theory'.

The Interviews

The first step in the methodology was to conduct, over an 18-month period between 2020 and 2021, interviews of 26 public sector leaders in Australia. Using an open interview format and style, I asked participants about their experience of responding to COVID-19, and about their leadership role.

In choosing my interview subjects, I considered the roles and types of leaders involved in crisis management, particularly those in the public sector who act on behalf of the government. (From here on, "participants" will refer to public sector leaders interviewed for the research study.)

Participants were recruited from a range of public sector organizations that were involved in responding to the COVID-19 pandemic. These included the Department of Health, the Department of the Chief Minister, the Department of Community Services, and the Public Sector Commission. I also recruited a variety of state public sector leaders, from Western Australia, Northern Territory, Queensland, Tasmania, Victoria and the Australian Capital Territory.

The agencies from which I recruited these leaders were also selected because they provided direct access to the most senior public servants acting as crisis leaders.

The stages of the research process are described in further detail below, covering the important incidents recounted by the participants that would form the heart of the data, the open and selective codes and concepts that were developed from the data, and finally, the theoretical codes that led to the theory.

Data Collection

The study aimed to identify the main concern for participants during the initial response phase to the COVID-19 pandemic from 2021 to 2022.

Data was collected over the 18-month period, with interviews conducted with executive-level public sector leaders across four jurisdictions across Australia. These leaders were either head of agencies or directly reported to head of agencies that were directly accountable to ministers within a government agency during the pandemic.

Interviews were conducted either in-person or via video conferencing, with virtual interviews providing flexibility in seeking views from jurisdictions across Australia. Field notes were taken for all interviews, and autoethnographic notes were also taken over the the period to capture my reflections on the crisis.

The interviews were exploratory, with broad, open-ended questions to help participants describe their concerns and experiences of COVID-19 and how it affected them personally and professionally. In order to increase confidentiality, and also make the participants more comfortable in sharing their thoughts, I conducted the interviews away from their place of work.

As timeframes for accessing participants were limited by the pandemic, interviews were sometimes planned in advance or sometimes undertaken when an opportunity presented itself (after professional meetings, for example).

In addition to the interviews, I collected data from secondary sources such as public documents, records, media articles, videos, and preliminary literature related to the effects of COVID-19.

Since I was also an executive-level public sector leader, I began journaling in early 2020 to capture my own experiences and perspectives, which contributed further data to the research.

Data Analysis

The data analysis process in this study involves various rounds of coding. The first round of coding is known as open coding. Open coding consists of analyzing the interviews for specific incidents described by the participants that could indicate concepts and patterns.

During the open coding process, 767 incidents were identified that seem to offer important concepts to help the researcher better understand the participants' concerns and response. Each of these incidents were given a code. With this methodology, the more you code, the more you begin to see the same conceptual indicators across the data. In other words, you start to see patterns and these patterns become concepts.

One concept that emerged from these incidents, for example, was the "language of COVID". Figure 2.1 overleaf shows a list of incidents, conveyed through excerpts from the interviews, that were coded as the language of the COVID-19 crisis.

CODE: LANGUAGE OR NOMENCLATURE OF COVID CRISIS

INCIDENTS

S0-2 COVID was a real event not an abstract emergency, allowing us to test systems and approaches (how we function)

C0-1 The language of war. Whether people chose to use catastrophic language – I used it – because

C0-2 there were no other words to describe what was happening when it felt like war

L0-22 there is perpetual uncertainty for the entire population and our role is to reduce that feeling

J0-22 even though it's like a war, it's not the same but sort of the same.

D2-26 ....it feels very much like a war – not natural disasters as these are finite

M0-3 like a train coming at us, and it was a real crisis

A0-6 it felt crushing, trapped and isolated through COVID from family

S1-1 I would describe it as an explosion of chaos, totally underestimated,

S1-3 like a blanket that smothered us

S0-5 we had no frame of reference to compare to, ..., it is different to a cyclone (a single event)

D4-3 it is a different kind of emergency with no spatial or temporal boundaries

N0-24 by comparison it felt like we were in a war-like footing in terms of politics

Figure 2.1

An Example of Incidents Coded as the Language of COVID-19 Crisis

Another concept that emerged during this phase of open coding the interviews was a concept that would become the core theme of the research: the concept of "public stewardship." Figure 2.2 below shows some of the incidents from which this concept emerged.

S0-2 COVID was a real event not an abstract emergency, allowing us to test systems and approaches how we function as public servants

H0-34 it felt like we went in like an army planning for war to protect its citizens

J2-1 role to absorb and shield the political pressure does not take things on that could be pushed to others

J2-6 found it hard early on and got upset about the impact on livelihood of people as we closed businesses down, people's potential future will go down the drain [from decisions] and was hard being confident in a decision

Figure 2.2

Incidents that Reflected the Concept of Public Stewardship

Memoing

How these concepts first emerged is through careful constant comparative analysis – looking for similar lessons that different incidents might share – and through memoing. Memoing is key because it carefully captures in words the insights and ideas that strike a researcher as they are conducting their analysis.

I used two types of memoing in my research:

- *Theoretical memoing* allowed me to establish relationships between concepts.
- *Methodological memoing* allowed me to challenge my own perceptions and clarify the results of the data collection and analysis.

Theoretical memo writing helps identify relationships, patterns, similarities, and differences, and delimit the analysis. The writing of conceptual memos leads to the emergence of theory.

As a novice researcher, I found the practice of writing memos from the beginning of the research process very helpful because memoing pushed me to write conceptually and not descriptively – which in turn helped me to identify concepts and to constantly compare data. By working with the data constantly – putting it down, reflecting, collecting, open coding, memoing, and collecting data again – I was able to move my analysis forward.

For example, hearing executives' responses to managing the crisis, I began thinking about whether their reaction was based on the context of the crisis or influenced by their leadership style. This led me to the concept of "leadership attributes". Figure 2.3 indicates how participants felt the crisis impacted their leadership style.

> R0-15/ 16 didn't change my leadership style at all during COVID but was more directive but was short lived
>
> D0-15 I become a bit more command and control – became less tolerant of the fluffy business and I did change slightly.
>
> A0-7 Lacked the ability to influence at a high enough level to make a difference
>
> M3-11 I became very operational, directive, nothing could be ignored
>
> H0-10 Visibility of leadership was important, people wanted direction and needed information.
>
> D2-1 in a broader sense I felt I could be professionally reflective and calm

Figure 2.3

Incidents in the Data in the Category of Leadership Attributes

Methodological Memoing

Methodological memoing (MM) accompanied theoretical memoing. While theoretical memoing was focused on the concepts and theories that were emerging from the data, methodological memoing was focused on the questions concerning the methods I was using. In other words, I used methodological memoing to put down on paper my concerns and thoughts about the interview, coding, and conceptualizing research method I was using, identifying any issues that concerned me as a researcher. Methodological memoing help me work out, for example, the timing of the interviews, what I should expect as the average interview time for a value-adding discussion, and what time of day or place would be most appropriate. I also experimented with when to stop talking, giving participants the room to move on their own beyond the original discussion.

Beyond these more logistical issues, I also covered in the methodological memoing issues such as the source of my data. I decided that I wanted to expand my sources to include larger public sector agencies, thus ensuring that I was getting a range of perspectives that would lead to concepts and theories that could be applied across the public sector, and not just one or two agencies.

The use of memoing (MM) also helped minimize my influence and manage my perspective during the interview process. This was a concern because of my deep knowledge of the subject area and personal or informal relationships with many of the participants. Asking open-ended questions prevented my forcing certain data to be covered, allowing participants to explore their perspectives without my influence.

In addition to trying not to direct answers from participants based on the information I had, I also wanted to avoid imposing my value judgements on what was being said in the interviews. The methodological memos helped me with this as well, since it is in these memos that I laid out my judgments concerning the issues at hand. For example, since I had expressed my perspective using the memos, I could maintain some level of objectivity when listening to a participant describe how a team functioned or how resilient that team was, I could maintain some level of objectivity even though I personally knew some of the team members. I had already diarized my perspective in a memo for future consideration. I did not need to bring up my judgments during the interview.

Figure 2.4 is an example of a methodological memo reflecting on certain steps in my methodology.

- I am also finding that as I interview people from different agencies their concerns and experiences are different so in order to reach saturation of concepts, I think I will need a broad public sector base.

- [I have also documented in the theoretical memos' reflections on my thought process:]

- I found myself leaving the chief Health Officers (CHO) coding to last even though it was done early. I'm not sure if it's because of an interview that was quite personal, or in a crisis such as this the CHO held gravitas in terms of opinion and much of the discussion included language re justifying some of the difficult decisions that had to be made, or I didn't want to influence any of the other interviews so I held back coding this interview.'

Figure 2.4

Methodological Memo in Undertaking CGT

Finally, through the methodological memos, I could consider the impact of other data sources and assess these in terms of concepts. For example, a secondary source of data was a survey of public sector leaders in Western Australia during the response phase of the COVID-19 crisis. The themes from the survey included service delivery, information technology, leadership capability, and resilience, as shown in Figure 2.5.

Service Delivery – The majority of comments reflected on the quick adaptation of remote communications technologies and processes to continue delivering services

Information Technology – Some agencies needed to develop remote working and IT security guidance and assess the need for renewed cyber security training

Leadership capability – The leadership discussion focused on effectively responding to the pandemic and how those in positions of authority were able to deal with uncertainty and change

Figure 2.5

Themes from Public Leaders

Note. From COVID-19 Pandemic Impact on the Public Sector May–June 2020 by Public Sector Commission, Government of Western Australia (2020).

The open coding and constant comparison can be somewhat mechanical; the methodological memoing allowed me to see my emerging thought processes beyond the pure numbers or language of codes, for example, looking for the intersections of different concepts. This process led to a concise list of the 13 initial categories shown in Figure 2.6.

1. The language of crisis and nomenclature related to imminent threat and war-like footing

2. Media, public discourse and political impact on action

3. Role of stewards as public servants

4. Leadership styles in crisis – effectiveness

5. Individuals' behaviours as leaders changing in crisis

6. The organizational role of structures in crisis

7. Resilience of individuals in professional and personal roles

8. Opportunity for change and momentum

9. Capacity for learning and growth

10. Managing risk of health and business

11. Teamwork across and in organizations

12. Impact on society from health to economy to education

13. The Balance of priorities- tensions

Figure 2.6

Initial Categories Emerging from the Data

Conceptualizing the Main Concern:
The Burden of Stewardship

Through the process of coding the data, identifying the key concepts that emerge from the data, constantly comparing and reworking the concepts through the memos, I was able to identify the concept of *the burden of public stewardship* as the overarching main concern of the public sector servants I was studying. The main concern is the core issue, what Holton and Walsh call the prime motivator, interest, or problem' at the heart of the research question (Holton & Walsh, 2017, p. 184). I found that public sector servants understood that in their roles, they were responsible for the health and education of society and the economy – in other words, they were the *stewards* of the physical and economic well-being of all the citizens in their jurisdictions. The weight of their role in protecting society – this burden – was deeply felt and expressed by all participants.

Resolving the Main Concern

In grounded theory, the foundations of a researcher's theory are two-fold: first, the main concern, which is the burden of stewardship, and second, a *core category*, which explains 'how the main concern is processed, managed, or resolved' (Holton & Walsh, 2020, p. 51). It is the most significant category developed that emerges from the analysis of the data, especially at the higher, conceptual level.

In my case, the core category evolved from the initial concept of 'making tough choices' to broader concepts of making decisions and managing risk before coalescing into the more focused concept of 'taking action'.

I now had the foundations of my theory: the driving motivation or goal of public sector leaders in times of sustained crisis such as COVID-19 was 'take action to address the weight of public stewardship'.

The next question for me as a researcher: What are the different factors that would influence the actions that public sector leaders do or should take as public stewards in times of crisis? To answer this question, I moved to the next phase of the methodology, which was selecting coding. Selective coding is the same as open coding – constantly comparing concepts and incidents identified in the interviews – but this time only focused on the analysis of data that related to taking action. (Glaser, 1998). It was not enough to identify these taking action-related categories or codes, such as 'making decisions' and 'feelings of imminent threat', but also to understand their relationships to each other. Eventually, I identified a list of 15 concepts (or 'codes' in the language of the methodology) related to taking action. These 15 concepts are shown in Figure 2.7.

- Anxiety on behalf of the public
- Imminent threat to safety
- Power to act by those needing to
- Public discourse or debate
- Team dynamics
- Organizational responsiveness to crisis
- Leadership style in crisis
- Personal characteristics of leaders
- Organizational structure that supported the crisis response
- Resilience of staff
- Trust in the government by the public
- Balancing risk against action and opportunity
- Burden of decision-making
- Teamwork for those making decisions and taking action
- Role accountability between different levels of the organization

Figure 2.7

Selective Codes Related to Core Category

Over the next few months, I continued to develop, refine, or expand on the properties of the categories, continuously elevating the theoretical level of the analysis while staying grounded in the data.

In addition to the data from the interviews, and my reflections through the memoing process, I also drew on additional secondary data sources, such as media statements, public documents and the survey of public sector leadership groups (Western Australian Public Sector Commission, 2020). These sources were reviewed to assist in improving my understanding of the concepts.

Eventually, the higher-order concepts emerged, and the selective codes were expanded to include subcategories that created dimensions on a scale. For example, the "leadership style in crisis" code was refined to include dimensions on a scale from directive to consultative.

This process led to substantive codes that described factors involved in taking action to fulfill the responsibilities of Crisis Stewardship, such a 'leadership styles – direction and consultative' and 'team dynamics, accountability, flexibility teams, agility'.

From the substantive codes emerged the higher-level concepts that would further help me to create the eventual burden of public stewardship framework. For example, 'leadership styles – direction and consultative' was part of the concept of 'leadership attributes.' Likewise, 'team dynamics, accountability, flexibility teams, agility' was part of the 'organizational cultures, teamwork, and role accountability' concept. The number of emergent concepts reflects the scale and global complexity of a crisis such as COVID-19. There are clearly a number of different factors that will impact the way public sectors leaders take action in response to the demands and expectations of their position as stewards.

Figure 2.8 lists the key substantive codes identified and the concepts that emerged from those substantive codes.

Theoretical Coding

I had the pieces, but how to put them together into a practical framework? The answer came through the final grounded theory stage for generating a theory: theoretical coding. There are a number of different families of theoretical codes (templates, if you will) to choose from. The family of codes that best reflected the relationships and integration of each concept for my theory took some time to discover.

Concept	Substantive codes
Stewardship	Burden of decision-making Balancing needs
Power to act	Trust in government
Taking action	Risk management, burden of decision-making
Crisis	Anxiety, imminent threat
Balancing judgement	Risk assessment and decision-making
Leadership attributes	Leadership styles – direction and consultative
Individual character	Resilient, fragile, sturdiness
Organizational cultures, teamwork and role accountability	Team dynamics, accountability, flexibility teams, agility
Organizational structure	Hierarchy and matrix organisations
Ambience of anxiety	Fear of threat, imminent danger

Figure 2.8

Emergent Concepts from Substantive Codes

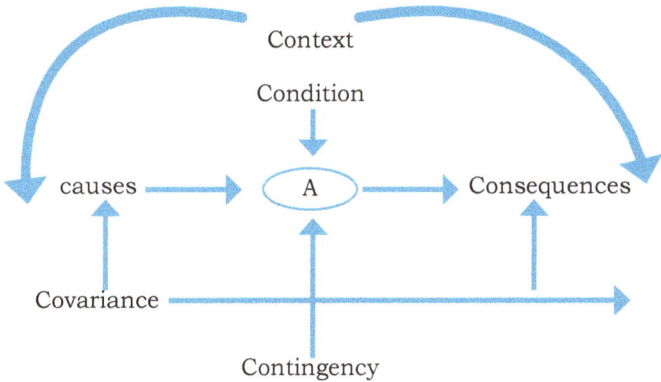

Figure 2.9
Glaser Family of Codes – Six C's

Eventually, I decided the theoretical coding family of the six Cs – context, cause, condition, covariance, contingency and consequence (Glaser, 1978 p.74) – were the most useful because they provided clear guidance on how to explain the Burden of Crisis Steward theory consistently with the data.

Although I had all the elements, it took some time to identify the structure of the theory and pull together these complex concepts in a less cumbersome way. Several iterations of the concepts were required, revising with each iteration the language to ensure that it was crisp and could be explained to others. Eventually, these concepts were fitted with the 6 Cs framework.

The following describes the six Cs family of theoretical codes and how they applied to my research:

1. *Context*: The context of the pandemic was one of anxiety, resulting from the information in the media and the resulting public discourse.

2. *Cause*: The unpredictable and inconsistent nature of the crisis was the cause of the societal anxiety.

3. *Conditions*: The conditions during the pandemic were tied to the public servants' power to act, which included: (1) the formal processes, such as legislation and policy, through which a public servant can take action, (2) the implied or informal power to act, which is the imprimatur of the public and the government that develops from the informal public discourse, and (3) the organizational structures and processes of decision-making within which the leaders worked.

4. *Covariances:* The covariances are specific elements that impacted the individual behaviours of individuals, leaders and organizations, and how they responded to

the crisis. Important covariances included the personal characteristics of the public sector leaders, and their leadership attributes. For example, leaders who tended to be authoritarian were more likely to have a more successful response to crises (including the COVID-19 pandemic) than leaders who tended to be more consultative and consensus-driven. Another variance often mentioned by participants was the organizational culture and how the culture enhanced or hindered the capacity of teams to respond when asked by the crisis leader to take action.

5. *Contingency*: What is the contingency that will cause decisions to be made and actions to be undertaken? The contingency in the pandemic crisis was that public sector leaders were expected by the government or the public to respond to the crisis – in other words, they were required to take on the Crisis Steward function, responding on behalf of the government to protect citizens.

6. *Consequence:* All of the conditions and covariances, which we will explore in detail in the next two chapters, would influence the eventual scope and breadth of the impact public stewards had in responding to the crisis.

Figure 2.10 shows all the elements of my framework in the 6Cs template.

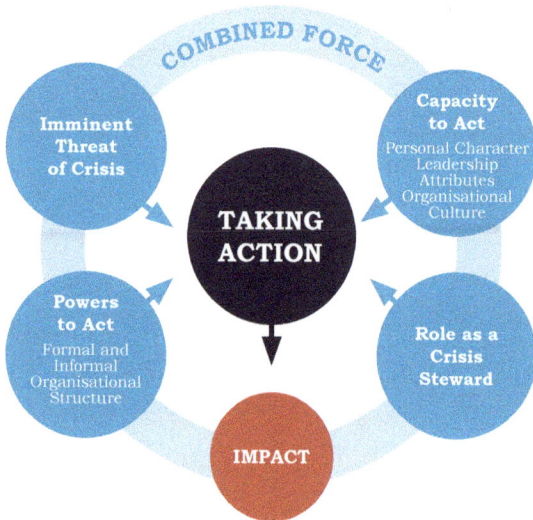

Figure 2.10

Elements of the Grounded Theory Using Theoretical Codes

Adapted from Theoretical Sensitivity:
Advances in the Methodology of Grounded Theory by
B. G. Glaser (1978, p.74).

With the help of the 6Cs framework, I was finally able to structure a theory that I labelled as the theory of *Crisis Stewards – Taking Action in Crisis*. This theory clearly explains the process by which the main concern of public sector leaders – to be successful Crisis Stewards – is resolved by taking action to manage the risk of imminent threat. Specifically, the theory describes the three sets of elements that align and combine for these leaders to take action:

- the *power to act*, which will be impacted by the leaders' formal, informal and organizational powers to act;
- the *crisis itself,* notably the persistent and unpredictable nature of the crisis;
- and the *capacity to act* which will be impacted by the leaders' personal characteristics, leadership attributes, and organizational culture.

In Chapter 3, we will examine the theory and each of its elements in depth, and in Chapter 4 how the Combined Force of these elements influence the approach and level of success by different types of Crisis Stewards.

Chapter 3.

THE THREE ELEMENTS

My framework, *Crisis Stewards – Taking Action in Crisis* describes the three elements that through their interaction as a *combined force*, will define how individual Crisis Stewards will take action in the face of a crisis. These three elements of the combined force are:

- the crisis itself;
- the individual's power to act;
- and the individual's capacity to act.

This chapter describes each of these three elements.

The Crisis Itself

The *Crisis Stewards – Taking Action in Crisis framework* applies to a specific type of crisis, one that goes beyond a single, isolated event. This type of crisis consists of a series of ongoing events that require governments to respond, and specifically leaders in those governments (i.e., public sector leaders) to respond as Crisis Stewards. The Covid-19 pandemic was an example of this type of crisis. It was enduring, persistent, and unpredictable, requiring an ongoing public sector response that had an unknown end time, and an uncertain resolution.

This type of crisis presents an imminent and emerging threat – in the case of COVID-19, the threat was on a global scale.

As expected, this type of imminent, emerging, and wide-ranging crisis created an atmosphere of intense anxiety. Eventually, as happened with Covid-19, the threat from a crisis can be seen as waning, with an equal reduction in the level of anxiety. The reason: the crisis is better understood as additional information becomes available, which assists decision-makers to make the right decisions and increases the trust of stakeholders (such as the public) in those decisions. Witnessing the positive impact of such decisions reduces the anxiety of stakeholders further, although anxiety remains as long as the crisis is ongoing. Clarity around any decisions or actions taken is vital: stakeholders may become more anxious and less trusting with any appearance of ambiguity, which can include new information or changes in proposed action steps and responses. In the case of COVID-19, the establishment of key pandemic rules, such as proposed business opening hours, and policy and legislation decisions, such as quarantine and public lockdown rules, border control, and mask-wearing, as well as expected public health measures such as social distancing rules, were seen as strategies for mitigating risks and thus reduced the level of societal anxiety – a major goal of the crisis response. For, as the next section shows, societal anxiety is pervasive in times of major crises.

Societal Anxiety

The emergent or imminent threat of a crisis leads to societal anxiety, the intensity of which depends on the level of the threat. This anxiety will lead to calls for immediate action to be taken by the "government", which means by public servants. These calls to action are transmitted through the media, public discourse, and individual comments expressed in every forum of social media and discussion. Governmental statements will also acknowledge the need for immediate action.

Finally, this wave of societal anxiety will hit individual public sector leaders not just at the professional level – shifting the priorities and urgencies of their work in government – but at a personal level as well, depending on their own circumstances. This personal impact will influence their response. The shared atmosphere of anxiety in crisis provides the context in which leaders receive calls to action, and respond to the imminent, unpredictable threat.

Responding to this call to action, the language used by public sector leaders reflected this atmosphere of crisis.

'COVID is persistent and unpredictable. Traumatic, dramatic and exhausting. Different to episodes such as a cyclone with a specific response', said one participant.

The behaviours of public sector leaders, and those of their personal, governmental, public, and media stakeholders, were driven by this acknowledgement that the imminent threat of the crisis required change, which contributed to an anxious environment and the resulting societal anxiety. 'I would describe it as an explosion of chaos and the feelings that occurred were totally underestimated', one participant told me in the midst of the crisis. Another said at the time, 'It is unpredictable and something might come but I'm not sure what'. These comments reflected the public sector leaders' own anxiety and sense of urgency as they responded to the increasing anxiety of government and the public. One participant said 'There was a sounding of an alarm quickly, with responses moving from months to weeks to days and hours. There was increasing anxiety and not orderly'.

The Power to Act

No matter the extent of the urgency and anxiety that push public sector leaders to act, there were three limits or conditions that determined just what action they could take:

- the formal power to act,
- the informal power to act,

- and the organizational structure in which the Crisis Stewards operated.

The interactions between these three elements resulted in a public sector leader's power to act in response to the crisis.

The formal power to act refers to the formal authority of the public sector leaders to implement policy on behalf of the government. This authority is granted by the legislation that governs the function of the agency for which the leader works. Thus, the roots of much of the action taken by leaders during the crisis were found in new or adapted legislation. The Western Australian (WA) Procurement Act is an example of legislation passed that gave leaders formal powers to act. This legislation allowed leaders to bypass normal processes so that they could more quickly engage individual organizations for assistance in responding to the public health emergency. Specifically, this legislation was used to justify quick action in procuring vital supplies to combat the virus, such as Rapid Antigen Testing and Personal Protective Equipment (PPE).

The informal power to act is obtained through the imprimatur of government and public opinion on actions to be taken by the Crisis Stewards. This imprimatur emerges or becomes visible through the media or stakeholder discussions, and is used by public sector leaders as permission to make decisions and take action to reduce the risk to the public in support of decisions at higher levels of the government. By utilizing this informal power to act to maintain the stewardship role, they are able to seek support for the formal powers to act, such as legislation.

The organizational structure of the government agency in which the leader is working is the third factor influencing the power to act. The structure of this agency or organization will influence the ability to take action. Some agencies, for example, are more rigidly hierarchical, requiring decisions to move through levels of leadership before they can be applied. Other agencies are hampered by a matrix organization structure resulting in public sector leaders facing several bosses and sometimes conflicting directives. Both of these examples represent structures that need to change for action to occur with the urgency required by the crisis. Such structures, however, are not rapidly changed – hence their inclusion here as potentially limiting conditions on the power to act.

In the following section, we examine each of these three conditions on the power to act in more detail.

The Formal Power to Act

The *'formal power to act'* of a public steward begins with acts of parliament, legislation, and statutory powers, which allow leaders of government agencies to act on behalf of the government. These agency leaders can then delegate decision-making authority to other leaders within the agency. In reference to public health decisions and activities, the power to act was drawn from the National Health Act of 1953. As the crisis hit, legislation already existed for dealing with public health crises, including the Emergency Public Health Act 2013 (Northern Territory) and the Emergency Management Act 2005 (Western Australia). Because of the crisis situation, public stewards at the head of government agencies had the formal authority from the government, through legislation and policy procedures designed for crisis contingencies, to implement these acts.

One of the goals of contingency legislation and policies is to allow quicker action than is usually possible under non-crisis procedures. For example, the declaration in Western Australia of a public health state of emergency was intended to give Crisis Stewards formal powers that they did not have when a state of emergency is not declared. This declaration, made by the Minister of Health, was authorized by section 167 of the Public

Health Act 2016 (WA). Another example of new formal powers to act were the changes made to the Western Australian (WA) Procurement Act, which allowed public sector stewards to bypass normal processes and enlist individual organizations in the response to the crisis. Specifically, this new authority over individual organizations was used for consumable procurement, such as the purchase and distribution of Rapid Antigen Testing and Personal Protective Equipment (PPE).

In response to Covid-19, every state and territory in Australia enacted legislation that allowed the chief Health Officer to enact statutory powers to take actions, such as closing borders and restricting travel, that were required to reduce the impact of the crisis.

It should be noted that given the imminent threat public sector leaders were facing, they had to balance the necessity of using policies and legislation available to them to make decisions and the expectation from the government that action would be taken without delay – which implied taking action even in the absence of some of the required legislation. As one participant explained, 'there was an expectation that we were being able to use and pivot policies in response to the situation as the default position for government'.

One interesting outcome of this expanded formal power was the implementation of changes in policy and legislation that were on the agenda for the government *before* the crisis. The COVID-19 crisis created opportunities for the government to move forward with these changes. In one state, for example, the government made changes in legislation for foster care so that family-based alternatives could be found rapidly – changes that the government of that state had been interested in before the crisis. These types of examples do not reflect an abuse of the formal power to act in any way, but rather the alignment of a need the government had previously identified and an immediate need required by the crisis. However, such changes often remained in place after the crisis ended. As one participant explained about the foster care legislation changes: 'Foster care moved to a risk stratification model for new kids coming into the system and a volunteer model for out-of-home care so mums could stay with children. The new model is still in place, with parenting training undertaken as an alternative because kids couldn't be put in care and this has been remarkable'.

Informal Power to Act

While public sector Crisis Stewards acquire the formal power to make decisions and take actions through legislation, they can also acquire the informal power to act when public opinion supports taking action. How much power public opinion is ready to bestow on Crisis Stewards will be influenced by the public discourse about the crisis, which occurs in debate, the media, and by stakeholders. Eventually, within a time frame reflecting the level of societal anxiety, this public discourse results in calls for the government to take action – or, at the very least, in expanded parameters of how much action the public is willing to accept. Such action may include legislation, but given the impatience of a fearful public, the government has leeway to use fewer formal mechanisms, such as easily modified policy or government directives. During COVID-19, for example, the government moved forward with the implementation of social distancing at two square metres.

An example of using this informal power to act was the public adherence to the guidelines from public health clinicians which was supported by the media and politicians, even when they were restricting for individual members of the public.

As the momentum for action builds, public sector leaders facing a crisis such as COVID-19 will be more and more confident in inferring that, informally, they have been empowered to act. As a result, they will feel free to make wholesale recommendations to the government regarding actions to be taken, or to implement decisions – assuming that those actions and decisions lie within current legislative arrangements for the public good.

The imprimatur of the public described above, which frees the government and by extension public sector leaders to take action, may be implied, for example when action is taken and there is little protest or response. Often, however, the imprimatur of the public is conveyed through the media, or through communication with legislative and non-legislative representatives of the government – communication that may occur through advocacy groups or unions. The media and other channels of communication with stakeholders and the general public can during crises help the government gauge the confidence of the community in the actions being taken by their Crisis Stewards. This was apparent during COVID-19, when the public and the media indicated widespread support for public health measures such as wear masks or increasing levels of isolation. As a result, these measures were rapidly implemented – and at times, were extended beyond the public health requirements because of the influence of public advocacy groups.

For example, the public, through public advocacy groups, became involved in discussions related to the implementation of the Astra Zeneca vaccine – discussions tightly covered by the media. This public discourse allowed for a consensus decision around a highly technical issue.

Organizational Structure

A crisis requires fast action, which is why the organizational structures of public sector agencies can negatively affect leaders' power to act: they cannot be changed or modified at the pace required to support the actions leaders need to take. The first responders to a crisis, designed to support anticipated crises, include regimented and hierarchical organizations, such as police, emergency, health and justice services. These are operational organizations, focused on short-term delivery of services and implementation of the tactical decisions of governmental bodies. A crisis such as COVID-19, however, also requires the involvement of organizations, such as Treasury and Finance, the Premier and the Cabinet, with matrixed structures, complex relationships with external organizations, and designed for longer-term and strategic decisions. Crisis Stewards must find ways to manage this mix of more agile and less agile organizations to prevent organizational structure to be an impediment in their efforts to respond to the crisis.

Crisis Stewards: The Dimensions of *Capacity to Act*

Crisis Stewards do not only need to have the *power* to act, they also need to have the *capacity* to act. A leader's capacity to take action is based on that individual's personal characteristics and leadership style combined with the organizational culture in which the leader is operating. The Crisis Steward's capacity to act, added to the power to act and level of anxiety created by the crisis together form the overall *capability* of a public sector leader to act as a Crisis Steward and have an impact on the crisis.

Let's explore the three elements of a Crisis Steward's capacity to act in more detail, beginning with personal characteristics, as shown in Figure 3.1

Personal Characteristics

Different personal characteristics are called to the forefront in different situations. For example, when faced with a completely unexpected event, some individuals will respond with calm and pragmaticism, while others might panic or freeze in uncertainty. In the context of responding to a crisis, the personal characteristics of Crisis Stewards that matter most include their comfort with change and their level of personal fragility or resilience These two characteristics can be summarized as *flexibility* and *stoicism*.

The spectrum of these two personal characteristics is shown in Figure 3.1. The flexibility dimension ranges from completely inflexible to completely flexible. The stoicism element ranges from fragile – individuals who lose their calm in times of stress – to sturdy, that is, less impacted by the stakes and urgency of the crisis.

Scale of the Dimensions of Personal Characteristics

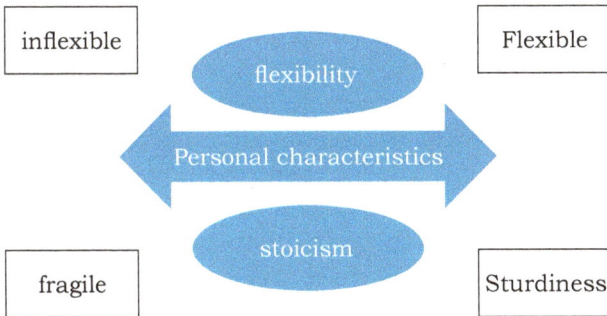

Adapted from Van Wart M., (2013)
and Bacon B., (2013)

Figure 3.1

One of the major challenges of a crisis is its inherent ambiguity: what is happening and what will happen is uncertain, and therefore, expecting to continue to operate as before may not be necessarily effective or appropriate. Some public sector leaders struggle with the level of ambiguity as they are generally less flexible in their way of working. These are leaders who are more comfortable maintaining the status quo, not only in terms of their work – happy with routine versus innovation, for example – but in their own lives as well – both of which are up-ended by the crisis.

Individuals with a high degree of flexibility, on the other hand, will be more personally comfortable with ambiguity and change. They are better able to manage their personal anxieties – since a crisis such as COVID-19 is not just a professional problem, but a problem that personally impacts them and their families – and are therefore less afraid to make key decisions in the rapidly changing environment of a crisis. On the contrary, these leaders are energized by change, excited about the opportunities for change created by the organization's need to respond to the crisis. Adapting and managing their individual concerns is not a problem.

During the COVID-19 crisis, we saw the effects of these opposite approaches in the inconsistent implementation of working from home arrangements. In some organizations, Crisis Stewards did not hesitate to modify and adapt their working processes so that teams could work remotely. (For example, they did not hesitate to allow employees to take work computers home). For other organizations, the transition to remote work was slow and painful, as leaders battled concerns of security and trust (asking themselves, for example, whether employees could be trusted to work productively away from the office, or trusted with work equipment at home).

The second personal characteristic, stoicism, which refers to an individual's ability to stay calm, resilient, and quietly resolute, is even more vulnerable in times of crises that can affect Crisis Stewards personally, as was the case with COVID-19. These personal impacts were serious, involving, for example, the health of family members, or their own health. Suddenly, the work decisions of these leaders were not just about work, but about their own families and their own personal lives. Not only had the stakes changed, but the interaction between work and home changed as well. For example, leaders now suddenly found themselves confronted by family members with their own opinions, buoyed by outside information from the media or other individuals, on what decisions and actions the leader should take. Because of all of this pressure, if leaders are unable to maintain their level of stoicism, they can become unable to function. As one participant explained, 'I had a panic moment, feeling selfish about my family and not seeing them, and wanting to, then I didn't think I could survive without them'. Another participant said, 'I would come home and have COVID-19 questions asked, I can't get away from it, it was there beginning and end of day".'

At the other end of the spectrum, public sector leaders acknowledged that they were personally affected by the crisis, but recognized this personal impact as an external factor that needed to be effectively managed. This meant managing the concerns and opinions of family members, and any potential complication or influence from individuals outside of their professional life. According to one participant, 'You had to manage yourself and what was going on at home and [your] own anxiety'

Leadership Attributes

As shown in Figure 3.2, two aspects of leadership will impact a Crisis Steward's capacity to act: the individual's previous experience in dealing with a similar or the same crisis – which can range from extensive experience to no experience – and the individual's preferred leadership style, which can range from authoritative to consultative.

Scale of the Dimensions of Leadership Style

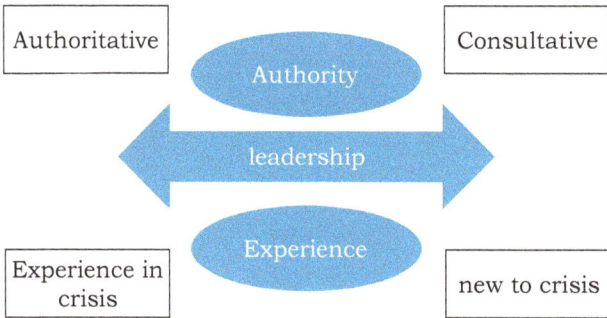

Adapted from Van Wart M., (2013)

Figure 3.2

Dimension of Leadership Style

The spectrum of leadership styles moves from the traditional command-and-control, solo-decision-making *authoritative* style of leadership to the *consultative* style of leadership in which leaders seek input from others and seek a general consensus for decisions.

Both of these styles are evident in the public sector, depending to a great extent on the characteristics of the agency the leaders work for.

Some agencies, such as those relating to fire and safety, police, and health services, require quick decisions, since these agencies are dealing with day-to-day, tactical and often urgent issues. Leaders in these types of agencies tend to be more directive or authoritative, comfortable making rapid decisions and taking action when required. In a crisis, such leaders can not only be decisive Crisis Stewards, they often seek to influence the decisions outside of their own agency where risk is anticipated. During the COVID-19 crisis, for example, police leadership in each state in Australia pushed for the implementation of border controls to limit movement across the country, although border decisions were outside of their jurisdiction.

At the other end of the spectrum (and it is useful to remind oneself that these are not absolute attributes but may exist in varying degrees), the functions of an agency require leaders who are able to develop long-term public policy through a highly consultative leadership approach, such as in the Department of Planning and Infrastructure. Outside of a crisis, these functions are not driven by quick-fire decision-making. However, these leaders have to adapt to the urgency of a crisis, putting aside their preferred consultative approach for more directive leadership – a shift that can be uncomfortable for leaders in this situation. For both styles of leadership, some adaptation is required to meet the situational requirements of a crisis when functioning as Crisis Stewards to take action.

Dimension of Crisis Experience

In terms of leadership attribute, the most significant dimension influencing the success of a Crisis Steward is prior crisis experience. Prior crisis experience is not typically a prerequisite for attaining higher leadership roles. As a result, even very senior public servants with extensive management and leadership expertise may have a range of experience with crisis management – from those with prior experience with a major crisis to those who have never dealt with a similar situation. Because a crisis of the scope of a COVID-19 pandemic is so out of the ordinary, experience with a similar crisis is vitally important to help leaders have the confidence and calm to act in the midst of threat and upheaval.

In contrast, without prior experience and given the ambiguity, heightened risk, and potential threat of a long-term crisis event, leaders' confidence will be shaken – especially in agencies that don't require urgent responses as part of their day-to-day work.

Granted, leaders are in leadership positions for a reason. They have attributes – the ability to collaborate or negotiate, for example – that contribute to their skills as leaders. That said, experience and leadership style are the two dimensions that significantly impact a leaders' capacity to act in the face of a crisis.

Organizational Culture Adaptability

Because of its significant influence on a leader's ability to act, the culture of teams in the organization is considered, along with personal characteristics and leadership attributes, a key dimension in a Crisis Steward's capacity to act. Specifically, the adaptability of team culture – whether it is rigid or, on the contrary, agile – can hinder or enable a leader's response to a crisis (see figure 3.3). The reason team culture is so vital is because of the impact that culture can have on how people interact and respond together to the crisis, and the support that they are prepared to give to the Crisis Steward.

Adaptability of Organizational Team Culture

Adapted from Bhaduri, R. M. (2019)

Figure 3.3

It is true that the level of agility or flexibility of a team is only one slice of the broader organizational culture, but it is the slice that most affects the capacity to act of the Crisis Steward. As one participant noted: 'You can't have a resilient team if some of the team members aren't in it in the same way'.

In agile organizational team cultures, team members are ready to respond to the demands placed on them by the Crisis Steward. They will work hard to make decisions as urgently as required, taking advantage of the team's agility to be flexible in their response – tailoring it to the demands of the situation.

In contrast to an agile culture, team members working within a rigid culture cannot or will not

| CAPACITY TO ACT | | | | | |
| Personal characteristics | Organisational culture | Leadership attributes | | Combination (key) |
Flexibility/ Inflexibility	Resistance/ Fragility	Adaptability/ Rigidity	Leadership style Consultative/ Authoritative	Crisis experience Experienced/ iNexperienced	Capacity to act
I	Fr	R	C	N	IFRRCN
I	Fr	A	C	N	IFRACN
I	Fr	R	C	E	IFRRCE
I	Fr	A	C	E	IFRACE
I	Fr	R	Au	E	IFRRAuE
I	Fr	A	Au	E	IFRAAuE
I	Fr	R	Au	N	IFRRAuN
I	Fr	A	Au	N	IFRAAuN
F	Fr	R	C	N	FFrRCN
F	Fr	A	Au	N	FFrAAuN
F	Fr	A	C	N	FFrACN
F	Fr	A	Au	N	FFrAAuN
F	Fr	R	C	E	FFrRCE
F	Fr	R	Au	E	FFrRAuE
F	Fr	A	C	E	FFrACE
F	Fr	A	Au	E	FFrAAuE

I	Re	R	C	N	IReRCN
I	Re	A	C	N	IReACN
I	Re	R	C	E	IReRCE
I	Re	A	C	E	IreACE
I	Re	R	Au	E	IReRAuE
I	Re	A	Au	E	IReAAuE
I	Re	R	Au	N	IReRAuN
I	Re	A	Au	N	IReAAuN
F	Re	R	C	N	FReRCN
F	Re	R	Au	N	FReRAuN
F	Re	R	C	E	FReRCE
F	Re	R	Au	E	FReRAuE
F	Re	A	C	N	FreACN
F	Re	A	Au	N	FreAAuN
F	Re	A	C	E	FReACE
F	Re	A	Au	E	FReAAuE

Table 3.1

Matrix of Dimensions of Capacity to Act

Note. This table presents the combination of personal characteristics using abbreviations. Flexibility: Flexible (F) to Inflexible (I), Stoicism: Fragile (Fr) to Resilient (Re), Leadership Attributes: Authoritative (Au) to Consultative (C), Crisis Experience: Experienced (E) to New (N) and Organisational Culture: Agile (A) to Rigid (R).

easily adapt to a crisis. This is why the degree of flexibility/rigidity is the most important characteristic of an organization's team culture, directly impacting the capacity of the Crisis Steward to act. 'In a tactical sense I had to manage across two organizations: one who responded regularly to crises and actually felt that they could and another part of the organization that couldn't' (K-23).

Dimensions of Crisis Stewards' Capacity to Act

In the real world, individuals are not necessarily at one extreme or the other of a dimension. They are not, for example, totally inflexible or totally flexible, but rather positioned on a spectrum of flexibility. To explain the dimensions and describe the interactions among the dimensions, however, it is necessary to use the extremes as reference points, and even then, there are 32 possible combinations of the dimensions relating to the capacity to act, as shown in Table 3.1.

In the following chapter, we will explore how the dimensions of the capacity to act synergistically interact with the two other key elements the *Crisis Stewards – Taking Action in Crisis* framework – the power to act, and the context of the crisis – to become a 'Combined Force' that creates the momentum for action.

Chapter 4.

THE COMBINED FORCE

Crisis Stewards: Using 'Combined Force' of Elements to Take Action

The capability of Crisis Stewards to take action and have an impact is affected by the elements we described in chapter 3: their capacity to act (which includes their personal characteristics, and leadership attributes, as well as the team culture in their organizations); their power to act, (whether formal or informal, and impacted by the structure of their organizations), and the characteristic of the crisis itself, such as the imminence of the threat it poses and the level of public anxiety it elicits.

All of the components that influence and impact these three core elements of the theory come together in what I call a 'combined force'. The combined force refers to the linking and integration of these elements and their components. The combination of these elements creates a momentum that is greater than the momentum of a single element (or component within that element), and it is this synergy of all the elements working together that determines how a Crisis Steward will respond to a crisis.

The 'Combined Force' in Practice

During the COVID-19 crisis, one example of how the 'Combined Force' synergizes the elements of the theory (the capacity to act, powers to act and an unpredictable crisis) was how Crisis Stewards responded to the pressure from the public to implement border controls to 'keep out the virus' in the different Australian states. These border controls created significant upheaval and personal distress as Australians under imminent threat from COVID-19 found themselves isolated from family members. In one state of Australia, the head of government received a very high approval rating for putting in place hard border controls, despite the personal impact of restrictions. How did the three elements of the framework work together? First there was only limited formal power to act, which meant the leader had to depend on a more informal power to act. This informal power to act resulted partly from the nature of the crisis (i.e., the imminent threat it posed), which led to a strong imprimatur from the public to take action, even action that created hardship in their lives. When the strong imprimatur from the general public was combined with the influence of experienced Crisis Stewards amongst police and health leaders, the leader of the state could create a policy that eventually kept borders closed to other states and countries for almost two years.

Another example of the synergy of the combination of elements driving action was the suspension of procurement guidelines and tender processes – guidelines and processes that are typically mandated by legislation. Building on both the *formal power to act* and their *capacity to act*, Crisis Stewards were able to use alternative Acts, such as the various emergency acts in each state, to overcome any legislative barriers to action. Thus, Crisis Stewards were able to ensure the supply of the services and goods required to combat the pandemic (e.g., toilet rolls, vaccines, PPE and additional staff for COVID testing or welfare call centre support).

The concept of 'Combined Force' that supports taking action is fundamental in the *Crisis Stewards – Taking Action in Crisis framework*. It is the combined force of the elements and not the individual elements themselves that enables Crisis Stewards to take action and do what is needed with the degree of impact required. Statements from the participants interviewed reveal the freedom of action acquired through the combined force. As one participant noted, 'We were authorized to do a lot when we had previously been restricted.' Not that such freedom did not take some getting used to. Another participant noted, 'There was a need to understand the timing and pace of decision-making and level of political interference. Some were more comfortable with that and able to use it.'.

In summary, the momentum created by the combined force – different elements of the framework synergistically working together – is used by Crisis Stewards as a mechanism to address their main concern: the burden of public stewardship in the face of imminent and unpredictable threats.

How the Crisis Stewards Framework Predicts the Scope of Impact

The combined force of the *Crisis Stewards – Taking Action in Crisis framework* can be used to predict the type of Crisis Steward who in a long and substantial crisis is likely to have an impact at the local, sector or societal level.

'Local impact' refers to the impact of a leader that is predominantly constrained to an impact at the level of the organization itself. Organizational leaders oversee and influence the organization through their capacities (personal characteristics, leadership attributes and organizational culture). For some leaders, the nature of their capacities enable them to affect the organization internally, but they never acquire the power to act to extend their influence very far beyond their organization. These crisis leaders, who are just basically 'surviving' through the crisis, are unlikely to affect either government policy or contribute to reducing the level of public anxiety. However, they can have some local impact by, for example, establishing business continuity teams within their own organization to manage any internal crisis response.

Crisis Stewards with sector-level impact can influence their own organizations, but are also able to contribute to achieving broader public sector objectives. At the sector level, such Crisis Stewards, 'striving' to make a difference, can influence decisions on policies such as working-from-home policies in the public sector, or revised sector-wide staffing models. For example, these 'striving' Crisis Stewards might be able to convince other parts of the public sector to share staff across agencies to provide cross-sector support for services to remote communities threatened by COVID-19.

Some Crisis Stewards have the capability not only to act beyond their organizations but even beyond the public sector. For example, the way they respond to the crisis can influence other sectors (such as private or not-for-profit organizations) who are also responding to the crisis. And their impact does not end with other sectors. These leaders can influence how the government reacts to the crisis and can also the influence the level of anxiety among the general public. In short, these 'thriving' Crisis Stewards will have a societal impact. One example of this society-wide impact is the agency leader in the public sector who influences government and industry leaders to push for change in the legislation involving the supply of goods and services. The result is that critical goods and services such as medical supplies become more quickly and more widely available during the crisis.

Figure 4.1 helps clarify what dimensions of capacity to act differentiates Crisis Stewards between those who have a local impact, sectorial impact, and societal impact. As shown in chapter three, the dimensions of capacity to act can be grouped into 32 combinations (at the ends of the scales of these dimensions), which means that the capacity to act profile of individual Crisis Stewards will match one of those 32 combinations. Figure 4.1 shows which combination applies to the three different impact scopes. For example, a public sector leader who is inflexible and fragile, who works within a rigid organizational culture, who tends to have a consultative leadership, and who has no experience with major crises (IFrRCN) is very likely to have the capacity to make decisions that have a local impact only. On the other hand, a flexible and resilient individual who works within an agile culture, has authoritarian tendencies as a leader and has crisis experience (FReAAuE) is more likely to make a societal-level contribution as a Crisis Steward when taking action.

Local Impact (N = 8)	Sector Impact (N = 15)	Societal Impact (N = 9)
IFrRCN	IFrRCE	IFrAAuE
IFrACN	IFrACE	FFrRAuE
IFrRAuN	IFRRAuE	FReRCE
FFrRCN	FFrRCE	FReAAuE
FFrRCN	FReACN	FReRAuE
FFRAAuN	FReAAuN	FFrACE
IReRCN	FReRAuN	IReRAuE
IReRAuN	FreRAuN	FReACE
	IFrAAuN	FreAAuE
	FFrACN	
	FFrAAuN	
	IReAAuN	
	FReACN	
	IReACN	
	IReACE	

Figure 4.1

Scope of Impact Combinations by Crisis Stewards Capacity when Taking Action

In sum, because different leaders bring together different combinations of components, the synergy and momentum of the combined force driving Crisis Stewards to take action will lead to different outcomes. That is, all Crisis Stewards take action in response to a crisis, but the breadth and depth of these actions and the extent to which they are able to influence others will not be uniform.

As shown above, crisis leaders will either have a local impact, sectoral impact, or societal impact based on their capacity to act. However, the predictive power of the Crisis Burden framework – that is, the potential for the framework to predict which public sectors will be most successful in responding to the crisis – is not limited to scope of impact. When we look at the *capability to act* of public sector leaders (remember that 'capability to act' is the combination of 'capacity to act', 'power to act', and the characteristics of the crisis itself), we find three distinct prototypes of Crisis Stewards that fully describe how and why certain leaders are more successful than others. Let's look at each of these three different types of Crisis Stewards in turn.

Thriving Crisis Stewards

The most effective Crisis Stewards are the *thrivers*.

Thrivers use the Combined Force of powers to act, capacities to act and the nature of the crisis itself (including the imminent threat it represents and the level of public anxiety it raises) to make decisions and take or influence action at all levels of society – from the specific public sector organization, to the public sector in general, to the society in which they operate. For example, during the recent pandemic, Thrivers were able to influence the government to change policies on social distancing and wearing of masks. Thrivers were also able to influence the public discourse on the different actions needed to respond to the crisis, such as adapting the original border restrictions when different types of travellers (such as returning citizens or those needing medical care) needed to re-enter a jurisdiction (nation, state or territory).

Thrivers have the self-confidence – and in their eyes the authority – to take decisive action. As a result, they tend to have more authoritative or directive style of leadership rather than being consultative. At the same time, they are decisive without being authoritarian to the extreme thanks to a more flexible personal style. They recognize, for example, the need to consult and collaborate with emergency and other agencies on the front lines of the crisis. For the purposes of clarity, the descriptions of the capacity to act dimensions in Figure 4.1 are presented in either-or terms, but it is important to remember that these are dimensions on a spectrum. Thus, in the case of Thrivers, one might say that their leadership style is positioned near but not fully at the authoritarian end of the spectrum.

Their flexibility combined with their decisive leadership style also equip Thrivers with the ability to adapt to the frequently changing circumstances of a crisis. They will rapidly take stock of what is happening and adjust their actions accordingly. This adaptability is reinforced by the personal resilience of their character: they are not easily fazed or overwhelmed and can remain stoic even in the face of the unexpected.

A more agile organizational structure and team culture undoubtedly feeds into the strengths of Thrivers, who have more freedom to make decisions and move forward. However, thanks to their flexible personality, they will find ways to take action within rigid organizations as well, although perhaps they will not have the same momentum towards decision-making and taking action as in more agile organizations.

The most significant dimensions for giving

Thrivers the capability to take substantive action is their previous experience with crises. Based on their experience, Thrivers can step in and influence the context of the crisis, for example by shaping the public discourse to reduce public anxiety and encourage more widespread support of significant action (e.g. changes to legislation) required to respond to the crisis.

Building on their experience, personal characteristics, and leadership attributes, Thrivers acquire, through governmental support and the imprimatur of the business sector and media, the power to act, resulting in a Combined Force that allows them to drive substantial action that extends beyond their own areas of decision-making. As noted above, the scope of their action, is therefore not limited to their own organization or even the sector in which they operate. Instead, thriving Crisis Stewards can take action that have a societal impact.

Striving Crisis Stewards

The Combined Force of their capacities to act, a certain level of a power to act, and other elements in my framework enable the category of Crisis Stewards we call Strivers to have an impact at the level of the sector they work in – the public sector in the context of the COVID-19 crisis. As noted above, Strivers' influence reaches beyond their own organization or agency. Strivers are the most common Crisis Stewards encountered in my research; both their characteristics and the moderate sector-level impact of their decisions and actions appeared to occur most often in the public sector leaders' response to the pandemic. For example, during the COVID-19 crisis, groups of Crisis Stewards found themselves required to make budget and financial decisions that affected the whole public sector – decisions that had each leader involved considering the whole of the system rather than their own organization. This extraordinary situation, resulting from the breadth of the crisis, was not in everyone's comfort zone, as one participant explained: "It was scary making decisions regarding finances so we had to make sure our spending was time limited; however, overall, everyone in group did what needed to be done, including diverting budget".

Concerning Strivers' capacities to act, it seems the personal characteristics of inflexibility and flexibility were not decisive in enabling them to achieve sectoral success as Crisis Stewards. Another element of the Crisis Leaders framework that did not appear to have a significant impact on the success of Strivers was their leadership style – that is, whether they tended to be authoritative or consultative,

In terms of leadership attributes, however, most Striving Crisis Stewards did not have any experience in dealing with a crisis in a leadership role. That said, they were experienced public leaders – a general experience in decision-making and action-taking positions that enabled them to stay stoic in response to the crisis even if they had never before faced the challenges of a major crisis. This sturdiness (as opposed to the fragility at the other end of the spectrum) is an essential personal characteristic when dealing with a crisis that has a personal impact not only on the individual leader but on the leaders' families and other people close to the leader – an impact that can naturally be distracting for a Crisis Steward and needs to be managed. A sturdiness of character also enables crisis leaders dealing with a new situation to bounce back from mistakes, and learning lessons from them to avoid repeats in the future.

This personal stoicism was one of two factors that worked in favour of the Strivers dealing with COVID-19. The second factor concerned organizational team cultures that were more agile and therefore more ready to support the leaders' capability to take action and implement change.

One example shows the power that personal sturdiness combined with an agile team culture can have on a leader's response to a crisis.

During COVID-19, two Crisis Stewards initiated the delivery of required additional and high-intensity COVID-19 support services, such as vaccinators for aged care and PPE training in classrooms. These actions were taken at the sector level, meaning that other agencies in the sector benefitted from the two Crisis Stewards' initiative. Yet the leaders of other agencies in the sector did not step up to assist. Eventually, public officials and politicians noticed the steps the Crisis Stewards and their agile teams were taking – with admittedly some mistakes along the way given their inexperience with crises – to implement the required delivery of COVID-19 services. This led the politicians and policy makers to push through policy changes that required other agencies in the sector to assist these two Crisis Stewards. These two Strivers thus had a significant impact on their entire sector, and not just their individual organizations.

Strivers' capabilities as Crisis Stewards are unlikely to have an impact beyond their own sector, however. Unlike Thrivers, they will not make decisions or take actions that would influence or affect the whole society.

Nevertheless, the sectorial impact of Striving Crisis Stewards – who, whether authoritarian or consultative leaders lean on their personal sturdiness of character and the agility of their teams – is an important contribution to responding to a crisis such as COVID-19.

Surviving Crisis Stewards

A 'Surviving' Crisis Steward is the public sector leader whose sphere of impact is generally focused on the local organizsation for which they are accountable. As noted earlier, Survivors will rarely influence the broader sector to which they belong or the society in which they reside and work. This does not diminish their impact at the local level, which includes driving business continuity for their own organization, and collaborating with other organizations to share staff in the crisis. They may also have a broader impact depending on the role of their organization in response to the crisis – for example, if their agency is accountable for the procurement of stock such as PPE for other organizations. It should be noted in these types of situations where the impact of the Survivors' activities extends beyond the walls of their organization, the work itself is still part of an extension of their day-to-day function rather than a substantial additional function related to the crisis.

If we look at the elements of the Crisis Steward framework, the dominant factor that keeps

Survivors from having a more substantive impact in responding to a crisis is their inexperience – which in many cases is not simply inexperience with dealing with crises in a leadership role, but even inexperience in leadership more broadly. This leads them to have a more consultative leadership style, which may work for them in non-crisis times but is less effective than a more directive style during times of crisis – when decisions must be made quickly and leaders must not be afraid to take the initiative. These leadership attributes hampering a Survivor's response to a crisis are not helped if the leader is dealing in addition with a rigid organizational team culture. The lack of agility in such a culture will not enable the Survivor to take action.

Survivors also don't have the personal characteristics that would give them the capacity to take action. For example, Survivors are more likely to be fragile in terms of the personal impact of the crisis; as a result, they will be distracted and cautious knowing that their decisions will have an impact on family members being affected by the crisis. Survivors are also more likely to ruminate over their own personal circumstances, which may cause them to overthink decisions and make them hesitate to take action. Even if they have the power to act – for example, if they have public support for decisions responding to the crisis – they may still not have the self-confidence to move forward.

An inflexible personal style that makes it difficult for them to adapt to change will not help. Although their positions in organizations make them Crisis Stewards, Survivors will constantly seek policy direction and guidance. Even if they have the authority and ability to make decisions that can impact more than just their organizations, they are rarely willing to make such decisions, rendering them less effective. As a result of all of these elements working together as a Combined Force – their inexperience, their dependence on a consultative leadership style, their inflexible and fragile personal styles, all of which is compounded by a rigid organizational culture, Indeed, Survivors can find themselves struggling to survive as leaders during times of crises. A typical example of a Survivor is the agency leader who wanted to implement a policy for staff to work from home (including himself). He was quite keen to put such a policy in place given the health issues at stake. Nevertheless, he waited till a policy on working from home had been implemented for the entire sector, instead of moving forward in his organization and setting the standard for the sector.

The Seventh C

As described in Chapter 2, the final stage in developing the *Crisis Stewards – Taking Action in Crisis framework* was to use Glaser's (2005) family of six Cs as theoretical building blocks – coalescing the previous concepts that emerged from my research into a cohesive theory. The 6C's consists of context, causal relationship, conditions, co variances, contingency and consequence, which fit well with the theory. In this chapter, we've introduced a 7th C: the 'Combined Force'.

The Combined Force captures the synergy and momentum that occurs when all the elements of the theory interact with each other. This chapter describes how the Combined Force leads to three different Crisis Steward prototypes depending on where individual leaders' characteristics and qualities place them on the spectrum of each of the elements. Figure 4.2 illustrates each of the concepts and the scale of the combined force (as a code) and its effect on driving action beyond the isolated concepts.

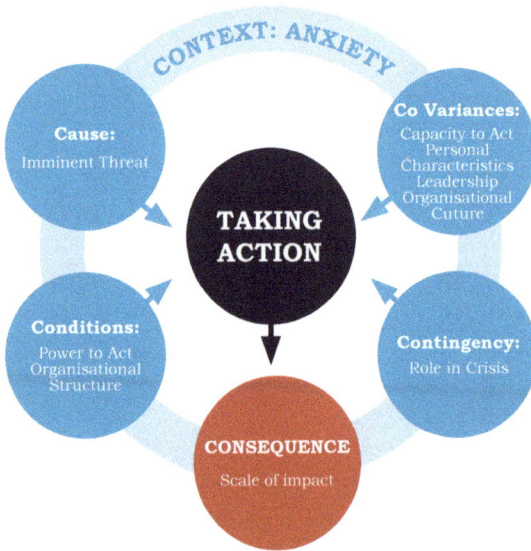

Figure 4.2

Theoretical Framework of Crisis Stewardship

'Adapted from Glaser, 1978, Advances in the Methodology of Grounded Theory Theoretical Sensitivity. P75'

Crisis Stewards – Taking Action in Crisis

The *Crisis Stewards – Taking Action in Crisis framework* is a dynamic theory – that is a theory with moving parts all interacting with each other. Out of this dynamic situation emerges three types of Crisis Stewards – leaders who must take on the burden of being stewards in the face of a persistent crisis as occurred during the COVID-19 crisis for public sector leaders. These three different types of Crisis Stewards emerge based on their capability to take action, which is a result of their capacity to act, related to their personal characteristics, organizational culture and leadership attributes; their power to act; and the crisis itself. While all Crisis Stewards take action, the breadth and depth of these actions, and the reach of their impact, contingent on the stewards' ability to influence others, vary among the three types of stewards. The terms used to explain the different characteristics of each group are 'Thrivers, Strivers and Survivors'.

Figure 4.3 summarizes the various characteristics, attributes, and situations that differentiate Thrivers, Strivers, and Survivors from each other. As shown in the illustration, the personal characteristics of Thrivers can be described as flexible (easily adaptable to change) and robust (or sturdy, i.e., not overwhelmed by the crisis). Strivers, in contrast, will also tend to have flexible personalities, but can be either fragile or robust. Fragility is a hallmark of Survivors.

In terms of leadership attributes, Thrivers are experienced and authoritative, easily taking the reins of the situation. Strivers are not always experienced in terms of a crisis, which may explain why they are sometimes consultative, sometimes authoritative. Survivors tend to be inexperienced and as a result consultative.

The agility of the organizational culture plays a role, with agile cultures supporting the Thrivers, while rigid cultures hamper the already struggling Survivors. In terms of the formal or informal power to act, Thrivers have access to powers to act, such as by enacting policy and legislation. They can also influence the public discourse surrounding the crisis, and often work within an organizational structure that supports their action. At the other end of the scale, Survivors are not given or are unable to acquire the power to act, such as through legislative change. Influencing the public discourse around the crisis is also beyond their reach. The Combined Force of all the elements shown in Figure 4.3 results in Thrivers having a societal impact, Strivers a more restrained sector-level impact, and Survivors only able to influence the response to the crisis locally.

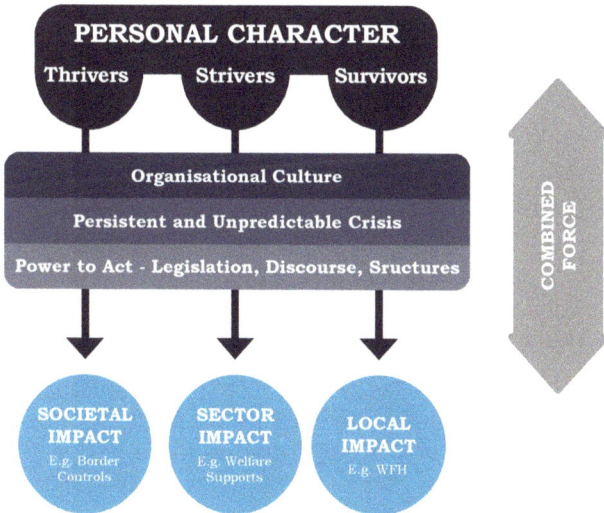

Figure 4.3

Crisis Stewards: Level of Impact Based

on Combined Force

Crisis Stewardship Summary

A summary of the crisis stewardship framework for those seeking to understand the elements that should be considered for success has been outlined.

The Crisis Stewards – Taking Action in Crisis framework outlined in Chapters 3 and 4 offers a detailed explanation of the elements of Crisis Stewardship and the 'Combined Force' required to take action for the stewards' organization, community, and society.

Ideally leaders who have been tasked with taking on a crisis stewardship role will utilize the anxiety of the crisis, their personal characteristics, along with the requisite powers to take action. The outcome of which is that there will be a level of action taken by them as effective crisis stewards.

FURTHER READING

1. Al-Asfour, A., Charkasova, A., Rajasekar, J., & Kentiba, E. (2022). Servant leadership behaviors and the level of readiness to COVID-19 pandemic: Evidence from USA higher education institutions. *International Journal of Leadership in Education,* 1–18. https://doi.org/10.1080/13603124.2022.2108505

2. Al-Dabbagh, Z. S. (2020). The role of decision-maker in crisis management: A qualitative study using grounded theory (COVID-19 pandemic crisis as a model). *Journal of Public Affairs, 20*(4), 1–11. https://doi.org/10.1002/pa.2186

3. Al Eid, N. A., & Arnout, B. A. (2020). Crisis and disaster management in the light of the Islamic approach: COVID-19 pandemic crisis as a model (A qualitative study using the grounded theory). *Journal of Public Affairs, 20*(4), 1–14. https://doi.org/10.1002/pa.2217

4. April, K., & Chimenya, G. (2019). Leader sensemaking in times of crises. *Effective Executive, 22*(3), 14–41.

5. Bacon, B. (2013). Intuitive intelligence in leadership. *Management Services, 57*(3), 26–29.

6. Barton, M., Christianson, M., Myers, C., & Sutcliffe, K. (2020). Resilience in action: Leading for resilience in response to COVID-19. *BMJ Leader, 4*(3), 95–97. https://doi.org/10.1136/leader-2020-000260

7. Bentzen, T. Ø., Lo, C., & Winsvold, M. (2020). Strengthening local political leadership through institutional design: How and why. *Local Government Studies, 46*(3), 483–504.

8. Bhaduri, R. M. (2019). Leveraging culture and leadership in crisis management. *European Journal of Training and Development, 43*(5/6), 554–569. https://doi.org/10.1108/ejtd-10-2018-0109

9. Boyd .M., & Martin E.C., (2022) Sense of community responsibility at the forefront of crisis management, *Administrative Theory & Praxis,* 44:1, 71-83, DOI: 10.1080/10841806.2020.1765288o.

10. Boin, A., 't Hart, P., Stern, E., & Sundelius, B. (2005). *The politics of crisis management: Public leadership under pressure.* Cambridge University Press.

11. Boin, A., Kuipers, S., & Overdijk, W. (2013). Leadership in times of crisis: A framework for assessment. *International Review of Public Administration, 18*(1), 79–91. https://doi.org/10.1080/12294659.2013.10805241

12. Boin, A., & Lodge, M. (2016). Designing resilient institutions for transboundary crisis management: A time for public administration. *Public Administration, 94*(2), 289–298. https://doi.org/10.1111/padm.12264

13. Boin, A., 't Hart, P., Stern, E., & Sundelius,

B. (2017). *The politics of crisis management: Public leadership under pressure* (2nd ed.). Cambridge University Press

14. Boin, A., & Lodge, M. (2021). Responding to the COVID-19 crisis: A principled or pragmatist approach? *Journal of European Public Policy, 28*(8), 1131–1152. https://doi.org/10.1080/13501763.2021.1942155

15. Bowers, M. R., Hall, J. R., & Srinivasan, M. M. (2017). Organizational culture and leadership style: The missing combination for selecting the right leader for effective crisis management. [in publication] *Kelley School of Business*

16. Breckenridge, J., & Jones, D. (2009). Demystifying theoretical sampling in grounded theory research. Grounded Theory Review, 8(2), 113–126.

17. Charmaz, K. (2014). *Constructing grounded theory.* SAGE Publications.

18. Cilliers, A. J. (2020). Leadership and stewardship during the COVID-19 pandemic. *Journal of Business Ethics, 169*(4), 687–702. https://doi.org/10.1007/s10551-020-04547-w

19. Comfort, L. K., Kapucu, N., Ko, K., Menoni, S., & Siciliano, M. (2020). Crisis decision-making on a global scale: Transition from

cognition to collective action under threat of COVID-19. *Public Administration Review, 80*(4), 616–622. https://doi.org/10.1111/puar.13252

20. Churchill, A., Barney, B., Hazel, A., Kelsall, D., Mouch, S., Dominique Verdun D, (2023) What is Stewardship, and should all great leaders practice it? *The New York Times in Education. Leadership Conference Essays.*

21. Department of Health. (2021). *Coronavirus (COVID-19) domestic travel restrictions and remote area access.* https://www.health.gov.au/news/health-alerts/novel-coronavirus-2019-ncov-health-alert/coronavirus-covid-19-restrictions/coronavirus-covid-19-domestic-travel-restrictions-and-remote-area-access

22. Giorgetto, S. A. (2021). Risk and crisis management. An overview. *Economia Aziendale Online 2000 Web, 12*(1), 1–12. https://doi.org/10.13132/2038-5498/12.1.1-12

23. Glaser, B. G. (1978). Theoretical sensitivity: Advances in the methodology of grounded theory. Sociology Press

24. Glaser, B. G. (1998). Doing grounded theory: Discussions and issues. Sociology Press.

25. Glaser, B. G. (2014). Choosing grounded theory. *The Grounded Theory Review*, 13(2), 3-19.

26. Holton, J. A., & Walsh, I. (2017). Classic

grounded theory: Applications with qualitative and quantitative data. SAGE Publications.

27. Hwee, O. B. (2020, June). *Stewardship in crisis. The notion of stewardship has never been more relevant today.* https://corporate-citizenship.com/2020/06/25/stewardship-in-crisis-the-notion-of-stewardship-has-never-been-more-relevant-than-today/

28. Janardhanan, N. S. (2021). Social stewardship can help managers identify novel solutions amidst the COVID-19 crisis. *LSE Business Review.* https://blogs.lse.ac.uk/businessreview/2021/07/23/social-stewardship-can-help-managers-identify-novel-solutions-amidst-the-covid-19-crisis/

29. Johnson, J. G. (2020). Stewardship and the COVID-19 Pandemic. *Journal of Business Ethics, 166,* 433–440.

30. Kapoor, N., Kumar, D., & Thakur, N. (2014). Core attributes of stewardship: Foundation of sound health system. *International Journal of Health Policy and Management, 3*(1), 5–6. https://doi.org/10.15171/ijhpm.2014.52

31. Liu, B. F., Shi, D., Lim, J. R., Islam, K., Edwards, A. L., & Seeger, M. (2022). When crises hit home: How U.S. higher education leaders navigate values during uncertain times. *Journal of Business Ethics, 179,*353–368.https://doi.org/10.1007/s10551-021-04820-5

32. McKibbin, W., & Fernando, R. (2021). The global macroeconomic impacts of COVID-19: Seven scenarios. *Asian Economic Papers, 20*(2), 1–30. https://doi.org/10.1162/asep_a_00796

33. Nolan, D., McGuinness K., McCallum K., Hanna C., (2021) Covering COVID-19: How Australian media reported the coronavirus pandemic in 2020. *News and Media Research Centre.* University of Canberra. Australia

34. Oroszi, T. (2018). A preliminary analysis of high-stakes decision-making for crisis leadership. *Journal of Business Continuity & Emergency Planning, 11*(4), 335–359.

35. Parliament of Australia (2020) *Update on Coronavirus Measures.* Media Statement https://parlinfo.aph.gov.au

36. Schmidt, E., Groeneveld, S., & Van de Walle, D. (2017). A change management perspective on public sector cutback management: Towards a framework for analysis. *Public*

37. Schmidt, J. E. T., & Groeneveld, S. M. (2021). Setting sail in a storm: Leadership in times of cutbacks. *Public Management Review, 23*(1), 112–134. https://doi.org/10.1080/14719037.2019.1668472

38. Seixas, E. (2021). War metaphors in political communication on COVID-19. *Frontiers*

in Sociology, 5, Article 583680. https://doi.org/10.3389/fsoc.2020.583680

39. Stan, S. O. (2020). Challenges of the managerial decision in the context of the economic crisis induced by the effects of COVID-19. *Management Dynamics in the Knowledge Economy, 8*(4), 419–434. https://doi.org/10.2478/mdke-2020-0027

40. Stobart A, Duckett S. (2022) Australia's Response to COVID-19. *Health Econ Policy Law.* Jan;17(1):95-106. doi: 10.1017/S1744133121000244.

41. Thomas, C. (2020). Decision-making during VUCA crises: Insights from the 2017 Northern California firestorm. *Journal of Business Continuity & Emergency Planning, 14*(1), 82–94.

42. Uhl-Bien, M. (2021). Complexity and COVID-19: Leadership and followership in a complex world. *Journal of Management Studies, 58*(5), 1400–1404. https://doi.org/10.1111/joms.12696

43. Uhl-Bien, M., & Arena, M. (2018). Leadership for organizational adaptability: A theoretical synthesis and integrative framework. *The Leadership Quarterly, 29*(1), 89–104. https://doi.org/10.1016/j.leaqua.2017.12.009

44. Van der Wal, Z. (2020). Being a public manager in times of crisis: The art of managing

stakeholders, political masters, and collaborative networks. *Public Administration Review, 80*(5), 759–764. https://doi.org/10.1111/puar.13245

45. Van Wart, M. (2003). Public-sector leadership theory: An assessment. *Public Administration Review, 63*(2), 214–228. https://doi.org/10.1111/1540-6210.00281

46. Van Wart, M., & Kapucu, N. (2011). Crisis management competencies: The case of emergency managers in the USA. *Public Management Review, 13*(4), 489–511. https://doi.org/10.1080/14719037.2010.525034

47. Van Wart, M. (2013). Lessons from leadership theory and the contemporary challenges of leaders. *Public Administration Review, 73*(4), 553–565. https://doi.org/10.1111/puar.12069

48. Walsh, I., Holton, J. A., & Mourmant, G. (2020). Conducting classic grounded theory: For business and management students. SAGE Publications.

49. Weick, K. E. (2015). Ambiguity as grasp: The reworking of sense. *Journal of Contingencies and Crisis Management, 23*(2), 117–123. https://doi.org/10.1111/1468-5973.12080

50. Western Australian Public Sector Commission. (2020). *COVID-19 pandemic impact on the public sector May–June 2020*. Govern-

ment of Western Australia. https://www. publicsector.wa.gov.au/sites/default/files/ Publications/COVID-19%20Pandemic%20Impact%20on%20the%20Public%20Sector.pdf

www.ingramcontent.com/pod-product-compliance
Lightning Source LLC
Chambersburg PA
CBHW040932210326
41597CB00030B/5275